OWN IT

5.5 Steps for Managing Your Career and Performance

SCOTT PATCHIN

Cover design and Layout by S.Y Lee-Wan
Editing and Publishing by Jen Hayes

ISBN: 978-1-7331346-5-1

Own It

A workbook with 5.5 steps to help you manage your career development and performance.

Who this is for:

Individuals who want to start actively managing their career and don't know where to start.

Leaders who want to initiate career conversations with their team, with the ultimate goal of each individual owning their career development and the leader acting as coach and teacher.

Achievement is talent plus preparation.
Malcolm Gladwell

,,

What it will do:

Provide simple steps that will help an individual get started on the journey of owning their career.

Why I wrote this:

I learned some of this the hard way. When I finally figured it out, and started teaching leaders to be coaches, I realized they did not have a road map to help their people step into the role of owners and drivers of their own careers. I wrote this as a simple tool that leaders could use themselves and give to their people.

Introduction
My Reflections

This was the first ebook I wrote, so I had a feeling this would need the most editing to convert it to a workbook – mainly because of what I have learned through my work with leaders in the years since I first published it. My original edition was focused on simplifying a very difficult process, which is stepping up to own your growth and development as a person.

Here are my two key learnings that are reflected in this second edition:

1. The first step – *Own It* – is the hardest.
I have taken a pretty intimate journey with over 30 leadership teams as an EOS Implementer™. We get to know each other well. I have seen 'ownership' displayed in a variety of ways and have observed the actions of leaders owning it over our years of working together. My realization is that I need to raise the level of vulnerability and make a stronger request for courage from people before moving on.

2. There is a .5 step at the end.
The .5 step at the end is the step that seems minimized, but this is actually the most important step. This is designed to be a journey – five simple steps that are repeated ONLY if you do this last one. I have to be transparent and admit to you that I spent the last year freeing up my mind and time to actually focus on my own growth. There are no quick fixes on your journey, and it will be measured in months and sometimes years. But I did it and I believe you can too. This step will get modified to provide you with a reminder and some support as you undertake your journey so that over the course of the next 1 to 2 years, your habits will become established and you will not need a reminder.

Thank you for taking the first step toward owning your development by making this workbook a part of your library. My only request is this: don't read this unless you are serious about your own growth and development.

This isn't meant negatively. We all have the best intentions but not always the capacity and mental space needed to take action. Don't waste time and energy on the guilt that gets generated by feeling obligated to do something when you just can't do it at the moment. If you are in this place, instead of procrastinating or feeling guilty, I urge you to share this with someone that you sense has the hunger and be their mentor. You will find this to be a mutually beneficial exercise.

Let the journey begin! ~ Scott Patchin

The definition of intimacy that rings most true to me is by simply breaking up the word: In – To – Me – See. This journey is about looking in, and the willingness to share it with others.
Scott Patchin

"

It was April 14, 2009. I made a lunch and headed to work early to prepare for some training I had scheduled for a new performance-review process we were rolling out. My 9am meeting with my leader proved to be the last meeting I had at that organization. I was home before noon as a newly unemployed person.

A friend helped me to put an upbeat spin on what had happened when he said, "Isn't it ironic that the person who helps others to build networks and manage their own careers is now practicing what he preaches?" It was funny, even on that day, and it was time to really put into practice what I'd been advocating and to see if it made any difference.

Prior to my termination, I had spent the better part of a decade helping individuals and leaders learn how to lead themselves and others more effectively. During that time, I experienced almost every conceivable organizational or professional transition. I call that experience the 'Employment Triple Crown':

The Hiring Crown:
I've been hired by someone and made the hiring choice on someone else.

The Promotion Crown:
I've been promoted to a new role and promoted someone else.

The Firing Crown:
I've been fired and had to fire someone else.

Your notes:

Through these experiences, I learned a few things about what's important in managing your career. The one clear message for everyone is that organizations can *support* you in your career goals, but it's not their responsibility to *set* those goals. **We must own our career and our performance.** When we do, good things happen.

What you will find here are the key steps for doing just that.

Step #1:
Own It

For three years, I was a lead facilitator for a career-transition program in Michigan called 'Shifting Gears'. We brought together 15 to 50 mid-to-late-career individuals who wanted to make a transition, often to smaller companies or to different industries. On the first day of the program, I could tell where these individuals were in the process just by their language. If I heard words like **they, them, frustrated, angry, stuck, trapped, can't** or any other word that indicated the thinking that someone else was at fault, I knew they were stuck. They perceived that the ownership of what they must do lay with someone else.

The first and biggest transition we all need to make is to shift our perspective. Consider what words you might use in your answers to these questions:

Who owns my career journey?
me, we, us, I...

Am I looking forward?
hopeful, optimistic, support, commitment, exploring...

Are my past failures an opportunity for growth?
I learned, I realized, I took away...

When we reframe something in our thoughts and start using words that accompany change, we show up differently. Owning it is a choice.

Without ownership, the journey is merely a path to prove someone else is wrong or to do just enough to get by, with one foot firmly anchored in reliving a past injustice. Assuming 100% ownership of your journey is the first step.

So, without me or another trusted coach standing in front of you and helping you gather answers to this very tough step, how do you do it?

Well, the mistake I made in the first edition was to just tell people to *Own It* and leave it at that. I have a core belief that individuals own their development, and organizations own the support. The problem I saw was that too many people checked the box as 'owning it' when they really didn't, and no real change resulted. The other thing I saw far too often was organizations providing no support.

It is a choice ... to buy into the fear and the system or to chart your own path and create value as you do.
It's your job to figure out how to chart the path, because charting the path is the point.
Seth Godin,
Linchpin: Are You Indispensable?

"

How to REALLY *Own It* as an individual?

First, identify your CLOUDS.

In defining what I call the Honest Culture Journey (*thetrugroup.com/honest-culture-journey),* I shared the four things that can obstruct your journey and cause it to fail, either through an inability to see, missed steps, or ignoring others on your journey. These 'clouds' not only obscure the path, but also interfere with our own ability to demonstrate the open and honest communication that is required for a successful journey.

Here are the clouds with a basic definition. For a more detailed description of the model, go to the back of this workbook.

- **Ego:**
  Too much or too little is the issue here. The key signs are statements like, "They can't..." or "They won't..." The net effect of the ego cloud on this step is that you skip through it without pausing to really think or reflect, either because you are too confident, or you don't have the confidence to be honest with yourself.

- **Fear:**
  It either has a paralyzing effect or causes you to make big, quick, and often reckless decisions without considering any input from others. For this step, it's about feeling safe to say it. Sometimes it is the environment, and sometimes it is based on a story we are telling ourselves. In either case, it is a barrier to the commitment needed to *Own It.*

- **Self-doubt:**
  Owning it takes courage. When we doubt ourselves, the courage needed is either not there or it will take so much of us to summon up that it leaves us little left for the rest of the process.

- **Crisis thinking:**
  The area of the brain that helps make fight or flight decisions is the amygdala. Beyond the amygdala is all the reasoning, thinking, and feeling centers of our brain that will be critical to the rest of the process. When we are too busy or facing some big problems, our actions tend to be very reactive.

Your notes:

On the next page is an assessment to help you put a number to what you are feeling. After answering these questions honestly, ask yourself two questions:

1. How ready am I to own this journey?

2. What has to change within me to make this journey successful?

I go back to my earlier statement:

My only request is this: don't read this unless you are serious about your own growth and development.

The clouds I mentioned above will naturally show up during the *Own It* journey, so we don't need to bring our own. I can still picture several faces of people I met during my Shifting Gears experience at moments when they owned it, and to this day they inspire me. If you are ready, let's go! If you are not ready, what do you need to let go of to let yourself be ready?

Whether you think you can or you think you can't - you're right.
Henry Ford

99

Make Your Action Plan

Here are some simple questions to help you step back and assess your readiness to *Own It!*

Ego

Too little			Healthy amount			Too much		
1	2	3	4	5	6	7	8	9	10

Fear

What stories am I telling myself that are getting in the way of owning it?

What fears do I have for the situation / people involved in this discussion?

How confident am I that I can manage the fear?

Low confidence / need lots of help			Moderately confident / need some help			Highly confident		
1	2	3	4	5	6	7	8	9	10

Self-doubt

None			Some / I can manage it			Too much		
1	2	3	4	5	6	7	8	9	10

Crisis thinking (of the situation you are in)

No crisis			Some crisis			Too much		
1	2	3	4	5	6	7	8	9	10

Based on your reflection above, how ready are you to *Own It?*

Not ready			Ready with some help			Ready!		
1	2	3	4	5	6	7	8	9	10

Resources to LEARN and DO more:

- *Do the Work: Overcome Resistance and Get Out of Your Own Way* by Steven Pressfield
- *Linchpin: Are You Indispensable?* by Seth Godin
- *Lean In: Women, Work, and the Will to Lead* by Sheryl Sandberg
- *Managing Oneself: The Key to Success* by Peter F. Drucker (Harvard Business Review)
- *The 7 Habits of Highly Effective People: Powerful Lessons in Personal Change* by Stephen R. Covey (Part One)

Step #2:
Cultivate Self-Awareness

It's easy to say, 'You are never too old to learn'. The bigger challenge is to never be too old to learn about ourselves, which means making vulnerability part of our DNA.
Scott Patchin

99

The economic downturn of 2008–2010 brought at least 25% of our working population to a point where mere survival became the primary goal. In late 2009 and 2010, the unemployment rate was around 12.5% and on top of that, the percentage of underemployed was estimated to be at least the same number. As a result, I saw far too many people defined by their circumstances. My conversations with people were littered with self-identifiers such as *unemployed engineer, frustrated project manager, ex-GM leader,* or *experienced professional.*

The economy recovered from that recession. Yet as I work with leaders, I continue to see people struggling with career choices and decisions. I still see people taking roles that are not in the sweet spot because they want the title and money – and then they fail. I see people holding onto roles when what they want from work has totally changed because of their proximity to retirement. They become defensive and territorial, the team tiptoes around them, and the outcome is an unhealthy and underperforming team. I could go on, but by not having an updated understanding of self, win-win situations become impossible to achieve. It is sad, and it often becomes painful for everyone involved.

Some simple truths:

- Age does not automatically mean we are self-aware.

- It is nearly impossible to be self-aware without experiencing some sort of trauma or failure.

- Self-awareness is useless if we don't develop the ability to shift our behavior to influence the outcome of our situation.

The work we all must learn to do is to understand our sweet spot in performance. Dan Sullivan calls it our 'unique ability'. The way to understand this place is to create that picture for ourselves around the three things that define us.

To know and not do is to not yet know.
Kurt Lewin

99

Our talents:

Those things that are just wired into our work; our gifts, strengths, and talents that emerge from us naturally. Examples include qualities such as empathy and a drive to achieve, and abilities such as connecting to people, or seeing a plan and making it perfect.

Our passions:

Those things that fuel us, that motivate us to get up in the morning, and that we hold as our highest life priorities.

Our desired rewards:

Those things that help us feel good about what we have done and often help us to endure the natural dips in life; that proverbial gold at the end of the rainbow which makes the journey worthwhile. The rewards we seek can be internal or external – ranging from satisfaction for a job well done to enhanced financial security for ourselves and our families – but they become the basis of many of our needs.

By defining these three things, we create a lens with which to bring our opportunities into focus. The challenge is being able to keep this information fresh as you pass through the stages of your life.

Research by Gallup and several other organizations shows that our talents don't change over our lifetime. In my work with hundreds of leaders and using / taking assessments of all kinds that are designed to help people understand their strengths, I firmly believe this. However, our passions and the rewards we want from our work do change. I have seen retirees want the reward of flexibility and seasonality in their work. I have seen senior leaders gain a passion for coaching / mentoring so they step out of senior leadership roles and go work in university settings. It is easy to find these stories; the challenge for you is to write the first version of yours. After that, it becomes the lens you view any opportunity through and a picture you will continue to refresh every year throughout your life.

Working hard for something we don't care about is called stress. Working hard for something we love is called passion.
Simon Sinek

Success in the knowledge economy comes to those who know themselves – their strengths, their values, and how they best perform.
Peter Drucker,
Managing Oneself

Make Your Action Plan

Define your talents

What are your natural gifts and strengths? Think back through your life at those traits which consistently emerge regardless of your situation or the type of work you are doing. Make your notes here:

Pinpoint your passions

These can change throughout life. Take some time to think about now – what are the things that drive you, that motivate you to get up in the morning, and that you hold as a highest priority?
Note your thoughts here:

Questions to ask yourself

Outline your desired rewards

These also will change throughout life, depending on your stage and situation.

Think about what makes you feel good about the work you have done?
These could be internal or external rewards. What helps you to endure the natural dips in life, making the journey worthwhile? Consider these questions here:

Resources to LEARN and DO more:

- *Let Your Life Speak: Listening for the Voice of Vocation* by Parker J. Palmer
- *StrengthsFinder 2.0* by Tom Rath
- *For Men Only: A Straightforward Guide to the Inner Lives of Women* by Shaunti and Jeff Feldhahn
- *For Women Only: What You Need to Know About the Inner Lives of Men* by Shaunti Feldhahn
- Any of the resources listed under Step #1

Step #3:
Create a Target

If you don't know where you are going, you will wind up somewhere else.

Yogi Berra

,,

While the exact detail needed for any plan will vary, having a specific destination in mind is critical to a successful career journey. Here are three benefits to having some sort of plan:

1. It makes it easier to ask for help.
Things written down can be shared with friends or key sponsors.

2. An end target allows you to set intermediate goals.
One of the top motivating factors for people is getting work done. It's hard to labor day after day without feeling or seeing any sort of success. Having a target and intermediate goals helps us feel success and provides us with fuel for the rest of the journey.

3. It provides a basis for change discussions.
Life is rife with the unexpected. Change happens. A set goal provides an opportunity to talk about whether a given change is positive with respect to our current goal, and how our work must change if we shift goals.

What Color Is Your Parachute (Richard Neslon Bolles; 1970) is one of the most popular career books of all time. Going through all the exercises in the book will provide you with detail about why you want to do what you do and many specifics about where you want to go. It will also take you many hours to accomplish the exercises and to achieve the outcome of creating a career target. That works for some people, but for others a shorter version would be helpful. On the next page are questions for you to consider and answer to help you create a target for yourself.

Make Your Action Plan

Short-term goals:

- *Option 1:* Where do you see yourself in 12 to 18 months? What challenges are you looking for? What problems do you see that you would like to help solve?

- *Option 2:* In your current role, what would you like to do more of? What would you like to do less of?

Tip: Focus on the problems you want to solve, not the title you feel you need.

Long-term goals:

- *Option 1:* What do you want to be doing in 2 to 5 years? If you had to create a career path for yourself today, what would it look like?

- *Option 2:* Take a piece of paper and using only pictures (no words), create a picture of you at your best. When you look at it, what does it say about your gifts and passions? Now, let's brainstorm a little: what are two or three roles we can think of that fit you at your best?

More about TrUst and TrUth from Scott

In 2004, I sat in a coffee shop early one morning doing some thinking on my career. It was that morning that the following two goals came out of my head and heart, so I wrote them down.

Career Goals:
1. Another job: Small company where I own training and am in a position to influence the business. The company has strong values, definite vision, competent and passionate leadership.

2. Long term: Work for myself in a cool role that aligns with mission, allows me to be involved with my family, and surrounded by people I like and that push me to grow/do my best.

The first goal was met less than 12 months later when I was offered the role in a 7-year old startup to develop the leaders to open sales offices in other states. It was at that job that I also served on my first executive leadership team.

The second goal took a little longer, and as I reflect on this, I actually have achieved it several times since launching my own business. I achieved it with my role on the Shifting Gears team, and currently I am living this as I work with my own team, my clients, and the greater EOS® Implementer Community. The truth is I could not have described my job today when I wrote that long-term goal years ago. But the magic of writing it down is that it allows me to review it, remember it, and live into it.

Keep in mind that creating a target for yourself isn't about being perfect; it's about being purposeful. When we articulate a goal, it creates an opportunity to work toward something meaningful. It also provides an opportunity to evaluate our choices, and to make changes where necessary as we refine our goals and needs.

Trust: Giving someone something they can hurt you with and believing they won't.
Trent Walker

Resources to LEARN and DO more:
- *48 Days to the Work You Love* by Dan Miller and Dave Ramsey
- The most impactful thing you can do here is to journal around the questions I present. I recommend pen and paper journaling. My preferred product is Markings by CR Gibson. The commitment is to do it two to three times a week for 30 days and see what emerges.
- *The 7 Habits of Highly Effective People: Powerful Lessons in Personal Change* by Stephen R. Covey (Habits 1, 2, 3)

Step #4:
Commit to Mastery

You need not see what someone is doing to know if it is his vocation, you have only to watch his eyes: a cook mixing a sauce, a surgeon making a primary incision, a clerk completing a bill of lading, wear the same rapt expression, forgetting themselves in a function.
How beautiful it is, that eye-on-the-object look.
W. H. Auden, Horae Canonicae

„

Summertime in Michigan is a time of art fairs and beach days. At both the fairs and the beach, I find that I lose myself in watching people display their mastery.

Artists who take you to a beautiful sunset or a forest full of birch trees with only a brush... that is mastery. A kite surfer effortlessly using the wind to propel herself over waves up and down the beach... that is mastery. But while it's easy to get lost in the end result, realize that the path to mastery is the *work.*

Malcolm Gladwell defines mastery in his book *Outliers: The Story of Success* by putting a quantifiable value on what it takes to acquire mastery: 10,000 hours. While talent is a critical ingredient to excellence, it is the actual practice of working those talents for hours upon hours that makes someone great.

This is a critical step, because up to now it has been about feelings and words. Now the work begins: 10,000 hours is roughly five years of work at 40 hours per week. However, when we're doing what we love, it often doesn't feel like work. When our work intersects with our talents and passions, it often feels as though we're sharing gifts – our gifts – with the world, rather than performing drudgery.

In the Honest Culture Journey, I outline the four key steps that get repeated over and over again: Clear Targets, Conversations, Pause, Re-Orient. Achieving that 10,000 hours of work requires all of us to break up our journey into smaller pieces so that we can see our progress, reflect on key successes and failures by pausing along the way, and re-orient often. In this sense, these four steps become universal rhythms for any journey that wears us out if we fail to note the progress we are making.

Whenever we set out on a journey to achieve a long-term goal, certain obstacles will get in the way of our success. The three barriers that most often infringe on our journey to mastery are:

1. Thinking too big and too broadly:
It's easy to get so excited about the vision and the journey that we fail to define the individual steps to get there (the actual work).

2. Getting overwhelmed or trapped in the detail:
When we stop to look at all the work required to acquire mastery, it can be overwhelming. A journey to mastery means accepting ambiguity and a fluid timeline as part of the challenge. The first step is to dive into the fogginess and start. Things will change. We must be ready for that change and not allow it to derail our journey.

3. Going alone:
There's a reason why world-class athletes tend to train in groups, and why entrepreneurs tend to find more success launching businesses out of incubators. We need the support of a community to handle the ups and downs of the journey. (More on this in the next step.)

The goals of this step are to recognize the work it will take to commit to and achieve mastery, and to pick two things to work on or experiences you want to have over the next year. It's vital to set aside time weekly – or at least monthly – to work on these goals. I call this our practice.

*Before enlightenment,
chop wood and
carry water.
After enlightenment,
chop wood and
carry water.*
Zen proverb
"

Make Your Action Plan

Here is a simple template I use to create actionable goals to help you on your journey to Mastery. Remember that on a journey you might select a bigger goal like lead a project team, turn around a company, or work at a startup. All the data points toward more frequent career moves and more of what is often referred to as a 'gig' economy.

Development Areas to Focus On

Goal	Measure of success (deliverable / date)	What support do I need from this group? My leader?
1.		
2.		
3.		

Another way to look at it would be to create a map to 10,000 hours. Here is what that might look like:

1. In 5 years, where in my life do I want to have achieved mastery?

2. What activities (hours by each) will help me get there?

Let me state the obvious – if you choose to create a road to 10,000 hours, it will take patience and persistence. The next two steps will create the support and habits to help you stay on track through your journey.

My story

At one point in my life, I realized I wanted to equip others for success in their work lives. The key skills I needed to develop were in facilitation and teaching. At that point I made the decision to say YES to any opportunities to do that with groups, and I also began to look for opportunities at my church, in my community, and at work. I have not added up my hours, but it is in the 1000s for sure. The key step for me was to tell people and to ask for help from people I considered masters to mentor me. The surprise that happened for me is that my mentors saw the capacity in me to be great at this and started to connect me with opportunities that they could not or did not want to do. After all, the people considered masters get asked to help all the time. I answered these two simple questions for myself, and my journey accelerated!

Resources to LEARN and DO more:
*   *Mastery: The Keys to Success and Long-Term Fulfillment* by George Leonard
*   *Jonathan Livingston Seagull: A story* by Richard Bach

Step #5

Find Partners

Through my role in Shifting Gears, I had the opportunity to partner with more than 150 individuals on a journey to work, sometimes involving significant career changes. By far, the prevailing observation I heard from participants was the benefit they received from the networking required as part of their work with us. For all the things these programs offered, it was the conversations people had with others along the way that made the difference.

A trend in leadership development as well as personal health has appeared in the last 10 years; the most common terms associated with it are mindfulness and presence. The universal truth is that when we increase our own presence and awareness in conversations, they become more than just words exchanged – because those words come with real feelings, perceptions, and back stories that make it a real connection.

These observations of the individuals in Shifting Gears showed me that, more often than not, support is the primary missing ingredient in a career journey.

When it is missing, here are the key mistakes people make when they first start their journey:

- **Journeys without support are harder:**
  When historic explorers have delved into the wilderness to learn or be tested – Sir Ernest Shackleton, Sir Edmund Hillary, Columbus, Lewis and Clark, the Pilgrims – they all had help, and they were successful (i.e., they survived and accomplished something). An entrepreneur friend shared an observation with me one year into his first solo startup: "I now have a better appreciation for starting a business on your own – it is hard! I much prefer having partners to work with."

- **Bringing support is about bringing the right people:**
  We know the answer; it's there. Sometimes it's just hard to see through all the life that's happening around us. Being questioned and having to answer can bring clarity. When we open ourselves to questions, the answers within us often emerge. Every journey should have someone to coach us, challenge us, make us smarter, and comfort us. Picking your team is key.

- **Yes, we are asking for help when we invite others, and that is hard to do – admit it!**
  Being listened to provides energy and stamina for us. By definition, a conversation can only happen when there is someone to speak and there is someone to listen. We all have bad days. In any career journey, it's good to have someone who – on those bad days – will just listen. Having a safe place to unload frustration or share disappointment is a well in the desert. The hidden fact is, they will also have bad days and being able to help others is also energizing! So this is a source of energy for you both ways!

These roles are not about having more 'best friends'. They're about intentionally joining communities of people in which you will get to know others who will see you work. We build relationships through getting to know each other, working together, and establishing trust.

The top two things you can do today to build your network are:

1. Assess your current network:
Using the worksheet on the next page, make a list of 30 people with whom you have strong relationships: friends, relatives, neighbors, people you've worked with. For each of the three roles above, where would each name fit? When you fill in all the names, what gaps are evident? Gaps are opportunities for action.

What does the list look like if you remove your spouse or family? If you remove co-workers? Are there too many Comforters and not enough Challengers? If so, you won't have enough people to push you when you get stuck.

2. Build your community/network:
Commit to two events per month where you get out of your business and your typical circle of friends and meet people who share similar interests or passions. Then, work with them. Examples of such events could include boards, professional organizations, chamber get-togethers, volunteering with your kids' activities, or forming a neighborhood group.

Leave this section with one final thought: this step is about intentionally cultivating strong and healthy relationships with people that will provide critical conversations along your journey. The added beauty of these relationships is that some will be truly reciprocal ones, and you will be asked to play some of these critical roles for others. In my experience of guiding and being guided, being included is like being given food and water: it will become your fuel.

If you want to go FAST, go alone. If you want to go FAR, go together.
African proverb

Your notes:

Make Your Action Plan

Own It! – **Partnership Worksheet**

Name	Relationship	Comforter / Encourager	Challenger	Expert / Mentor	Door Opener / Connector
1.					
2					
3.					
4.					
5.					
6.					
7.					
8.					
9.					
10.					
11.					

Accountability Partner	Coach / Questioner	Listener					

Resources to LEARN and DO more:

- See journaling comment in the previous step. Focus on the two things you can do today to build your network from this workbook.
- *The 7 Habits of Highly Effective People: Powerful Lessons in Personal Change* by Stephen R. Covey (Habits 4, 5, 6)

Step #5.5

Hone the Habits

Once you have completed these five steps, it's now time to synthesize, review, revise, and repeat. Practice makes perfect. .

Some of the great minds in personal development have used varying terms for this step, but the content is essentially the same. Stephen Covey called it 'sharpening the saw'. Peter Drucker called it 'feedback analysis'.

As I mentioned in the introduction, this is the one step I see people fail to do because they get busy and comfortable, and this becomes one of those tasks to be done later. The problem is – you becoming your best takes intentionality.

This step is about making time to revisit some of the plans you have set for yourself, the things you have defined as priorities, and the items that created a picture of you at your best: your talents, passions, and desired rewards. Revisit these points and update them based on what you have learned.

Time does change and refine things. Life events such as death or divorce may happen, necessitating a shift in priorities or needs. When we take on challenging projects, we experience times of success and of failure, both of which help us refine what we know about ourselves.

A bird doesn't sing because it has an answer, it sings because it has a song.
Maya Angelou

Make Your Action Plan

In his article *Managing Oneself,* Peter Drucker describes how reflective journaling refines the self-knowledge that is so critical for a worker in the new economy.

The key habits here are:

1. Writing down your plans, including:

    • What do you know about yourself?

    • What experiences do you want to have in the next 12-18 months?

    • Where do you see yourself in 2 to 5 years?

2. Carve out 1 to 8 hours once or twice per year to revisit and revise some of your plans.

Resources to LEARN and DO more:
•   See journaling comment in the previous step. Use the questions here in the workbook.
•   *The 7 Habits of Highly Effective People: Powerful Lessons in Personal Change* by Stephen R. Covey (Habits 7)

One thing that I've learned over my career is that everyone has amazing gifts to bring to the world. These gifts can make an incredible difference in the organizations you join, but in order to make that match there has to be a great conversation. What you bring to the table is knowledge of yourself created by owning the process of development and self-discovery.

Go Own It!

Your Planning Framework

The Honest Culture Journey

Plans help leaders move the organization, but being involved in the planning is the key step in getting the 21st century team member to own it and drive it. If you want extra passion and effort, include them!

Scott Patchin

99

Strategic planning is a journey. Using the lens of honest culture to manage it will make the outcomes so much more powerful and the journey so much more energizing.

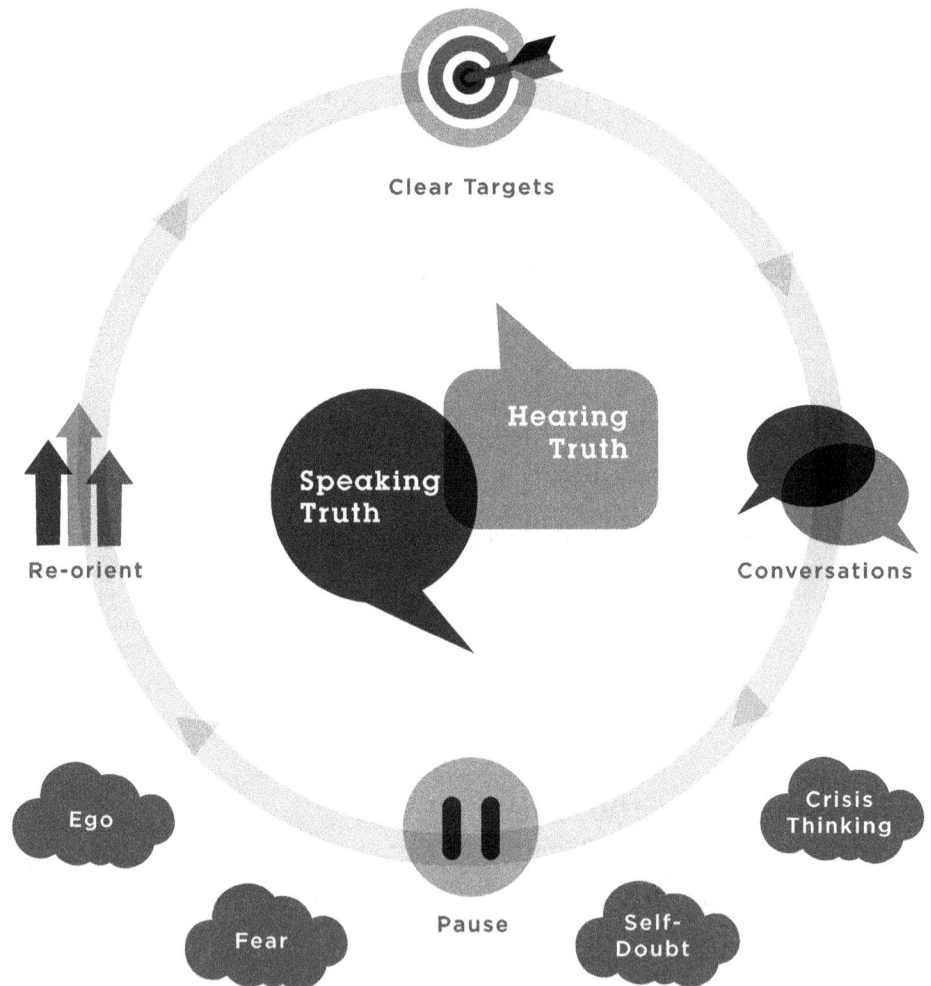

Clear Targets

Re-orient

Speaking Truth

Hearing Truth

Conversations

Ego

Fear

Pause

Self-Doubt

Crisis Thinking

The center of the Honest Culture Journey is speaking truth and hearing truth. This is at the heart of the work. To the extent it happens, the journey becomes a place where respect is given and felt, which is a key ingredient to a healthy and high-performing team. Trust and respect are accelerators to success.

To get you started, here is how the key events go together:

Clear Targets

Every journey has a destination – whether it is physical, spiritual, or emotional. There is always a reason. When a team is involved, it provides the foundation for the relationships from the very beginning. It starts with the simple question: "Why are we doing this?" Then it gets to the other key pieces of information – the who? what? where? when? and how? of our journey. There are two more key questions to answer, but this gets us started.

Conversations

Our journey joins the need to achieve something and the relationship outcome of doing it as a team. This step is about all the interactions that just happen when we journey together. Things like same room/same time connections, instant texts or emails, or even slow connections such as dangling texts, unresolved emails, or other barriers to our sense of immediacy.

Pause

Journeys are fraught with movement, emotions, shortages, and lots of rerouting. The pause is an intentional event to slow down and focus people on speaking truth and, even more importantly, hearing truth. It can be a one-to-one, leader-to-many, or a team pause (three to eight people). There is no time limit, only the objective to quiet the noise of the journey to speak and hear truth from each other. An effective pause creates an emotionally safe place for all to share and a physical space to allow all to focus.

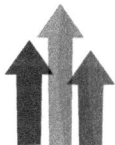

Re-orient

Effective journeys go beyond the simple question of "Are we there yet?" to the powerful questions of "How far have we gone?" and "What will it take to finish the journey?" This step is the action step after the pause to reset the picture of what? where? when? and how? with the most critical step to assign or reassign the who? involved. As roles and tasks shift on a journey, it is important for all teams and individuals to have clarity and alignment on the work ahead. Reorient makes sure that happens.

There are four things that will obstruct your journey and cause it to fail, either through an inability to see, missed steps, or ignoring others on your journey. I call these clouds, and they come in four forms:

Ego: Too much or too little is the issue here. The key signs are statements like, "They can't..." or "They won't..."

Fear: It either has a paralyzing effect or causes you to make big, quick, and often reckless decisions without considering any input from others.

Self-doubt: It can sound a lot like too little Ego, but the biggest challenge is getting people to speak up and share. This cloud causes people to disappear.

Crisis thinking: It is often rooted in fear, and moves decision-making to the amygdala or, as Seth Godin calls it, 'The Lizard Brain'. This is most commonly called the 'fight-or-flight' response.

Visit thetrugroup.com/honest-culture-journey to learn more about the tools I have created to equip you for this journey and to get on a list to hear more.

www.ingramcontent.com/pod-product-compliance
Lightning Source LLC
Chambersburg PA
CBHW051405200326
41520CB00024B/7505